READING POWER

UNICEF

United Nations Children's Fund

Anastasia Suen

The Rosen Publishing Group's
PowerKids Press™
New York

Published in 2002 by The Rosen Publishing Group, Inc.
29 East 21st Street, New York, NY 10010

First Edition

Book Design: Michelle Innes

Photo Credits: Cover, pp. 6–10, 12–13, 15–21 © UNICEF; pp. 4–5 © Corbis

Suen, Anastasia.
UNICEF / Anastasia Suen.
    p. cm. — (Helping organizations)
Includes bibliographical references and index.
ISBN 0-8239-6005-6
1. UNICEF—Juvenile literature. [1. UNICEF.]   I. Title.
HV703 .S84 2002
362.7—dc21

                                    2001000608

Manufactured in the United States of America

Contents

What Is UNICEF?

In 1945, fifty-one nations got together at the end of World War II. They wanted to keep peace in the world. They started the United Nations.

In 1946, the United Nations started UNICEF. UNICEF stands for "United Nations Children's Fund."

The United Nations building is in New York City.

Many countries give money to UNICEF. UNICEF uses the money it gets to help families all over the world.

The Most Money Given to UNICEF in 1999	
Country	Amount
United States	$205 million
Sweden	$70 million
Japan	$65 million

A woman smiles at her child in the country of Myanmar in Southeast Asia.

Children also help raise money for UNICEF. In 1950, a youth group in Philadelphia, Pennsylvania, collected $17 for UNICEF while trick-or-treating.

Now, many young people all across the United States and Canada trick-or-treat for UNICEF.

9

UNICEF Holiday Cards

UNICEF also sells holiday cards to raise money. The first card was made in 1947. It showed a painting by a seven-year-old girl from Czechoslovakia. She sent her painting to UNICEF as a thank-you for helping her after a war.

 This is the first UNICEF holiday card.

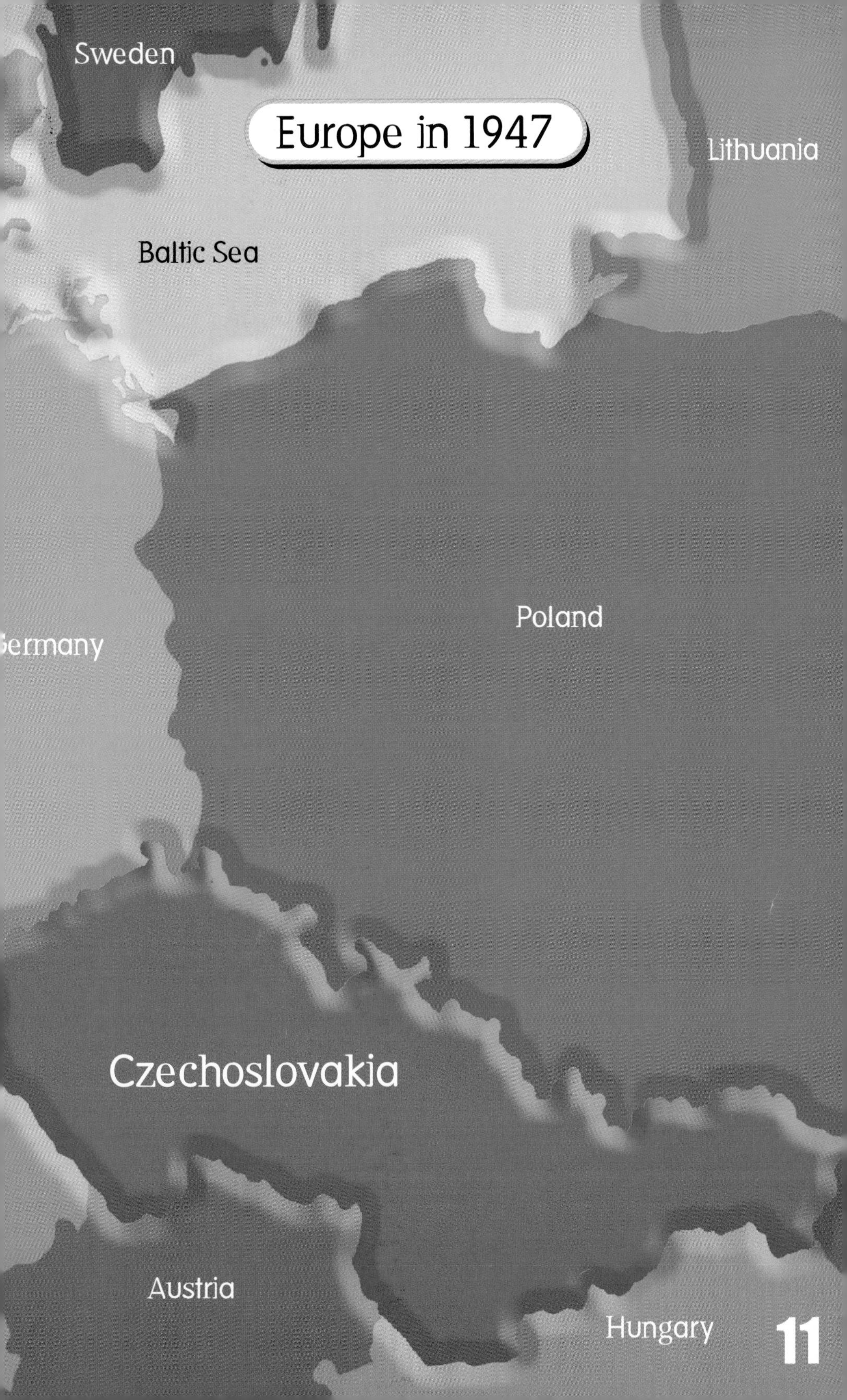

Europe in 1947

Sweden

Lithuania

Baltic Sea

Germany

Poland

Czechoslovakia

Austria

Hungary

11

Every year, students between six and thirteen years old can enter the UNICEF card contest. In 1999, the two winners were seven and ten years old. Almost two and one-half million cards were sold that year. The holiday cards raised $12 million for UNICEF.

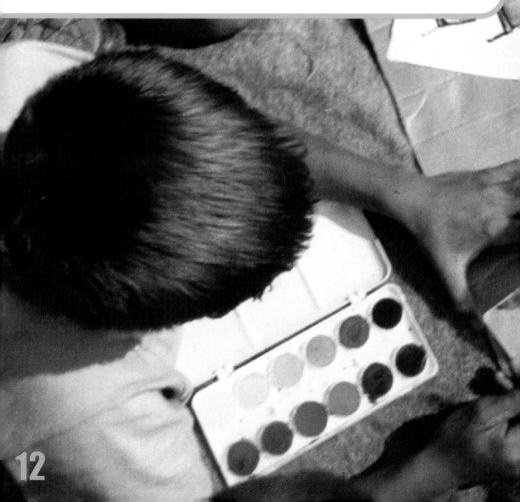

It's a Fact

Money from the sale of one card can help a sick child for two weeks.

Today, UNICEF works in 161 countries. In one year, UNICEF helps more than seven million children around the world.

A man in Haiti feeds his baby girl a cup of special food.

In March 2000, there was a bad flood in South Africa. People were left without food or places to live. UNICEF sent food and medicine to the children there.

Volunteers deliver supplies to people in South Africa.

UNICEF helps children in other ways, too. UNICEF gives children toys and school supplies. It also helps children get books for school.

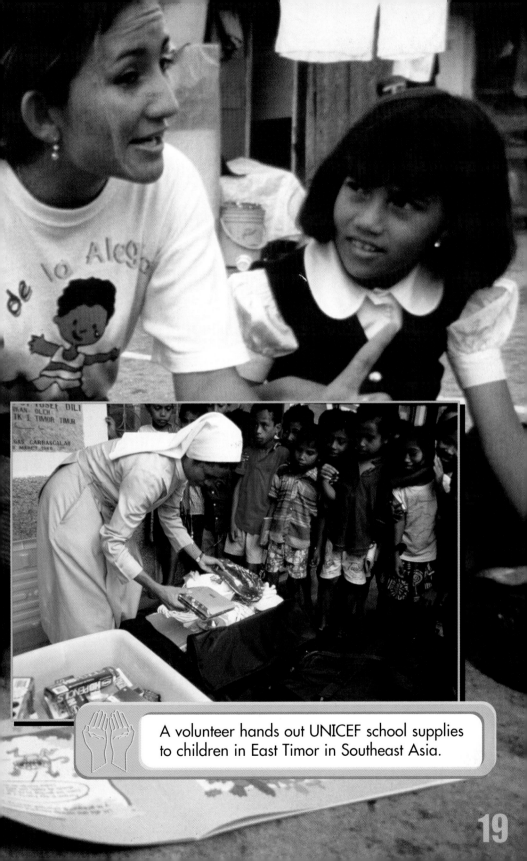

A volunteer hands out UNICEF school supplies to children in East Timor in Southeast Asia.

UNICEF helps children all over the world stay happy and healthy.

Glossary

contest (**kahn**-tehst) a competition between two or more people for a prize

countries (**kuhn**-treez) groups of people who share the same land and government

Czechoslovakia (chehk-uh-sloh-**vah**-kee-uh) the old name for the countries now called the Czech Republic and Slovakia

flood (**fluhd**) a great flow of water over an area

nations (**nay**-shuhnz) groups of people who share the same land and government

united (yoo-**ny**-tihd) joined together for one purpose

United Nations (yoo-**ny**-tihd **nay**-shuhnz) a group of countries that work together for peace, understanding, and world progress

Resources

Books

Children Just Like Me
by Susan E. Copsey, Anabel Kindersley, and
Barnabus Kindersley
Dorling Kindersley Publishing (1995)

*For Every Child: The Rights of the Child in
Words and Pictures*
adapted by Caroline Castle
Putnam/Fogelman (2000)

Web Site
http://www.unicef.org/young/

Index

Word Count: 285

Note to Librarians, Teachers, and Parents

    If reading is a challenge, Reading Power is a solution! Reading Power is perfect for readers who want high-interest subject matter at an accessible reading level. These fact-filled, photo-illustrated books are designed for readers who want straightforward vocabulary, engaging topics, and a manageable reading experience. With clear picture/text correspondence, leveled Reading Power books put the reader in charge. Now readers have the power to get the information they want and the skills they need in a user-friendly format.